MW01488968

thoughts of a teenage girl.

thoughts of

a teenage

girl.

katherine mazzei

thoughts of a teenage girl.

dedication

for all the teens out there, who are
confused, hurt, angry, sad, and just want to
be happy. just know you are not alone.

thoughts of a teenage girl.

table of contents

thoughts of a teenage girl.

author's note

this should be a book
about hurt
and
about growth.

but i don't know
how to grow just yet.

so, live with me
through the hurt for a while
and maybe someday
you can be there for the healing.

thoughts of a teenage girl playlist

society

society — eddie vedder
stressed out — twenty one pilots
bullet with butterfly wings — the smashing pumpkins
all-american b*tch — olivia rodrigo
longview — green day
one — johnny cash
bad reputation — joan jett

doubt

teenage dream — olivia rodrigo
out of the woods — taylor swift
give me novacaine — green day
the great war — taylor swift

pain

hurt — johnny cash
iris — goo goo dolls
wake me up when september ends— green day
is it over now? — taylor swift

9

would've, could've, should've —
taylor swift
you're on your own kid — taylor swift
creep — radiohead
boulevard of broken dreams — green day
this is me trying — taylor swift

dreams

dreams — fleetwood mac
wildest dreams — taylor swift
fade into you — mazzy star
mean — taylor swift
slut! — taylor swift
labyrinth — taylor swift
runnin' down a dream — tom petty
wonderwall — oasis

reality

anti-hero — taylor swift
just a girl — no doubt
the kids aren't alright — the offspring
smells like teen spirit — nirvana

ballad of a homeschooled girl —
olivia rodrigo
a place in this world — taylor swift
pretty isn't pretty — olivia rodrigo
extraordinary girl — green day
loser — beck

*(to access the playlist on Spotify, feel free to
scan the code below :)*

foreword

Hello, my name is Katherine Mazzei and this is my book.

I have always dreamed of writing a book, but with every attempt I made, it never work out. Currently, I am sixteen years old and, in all reality, haven't had the chance to experience a lot of things in life. From the start, I wanted to write something that I knew, something that was within me, so I bring you, *thoughts of a teenage girl*.

My goal for this book was to express how I truly feel about life as a teenager in our world today, and though I tend to be quiet around people at school, I really have a lot to say. In 2020, I decided to begin journaling and took everything that I was feeling and formed them into words. In my junior year of high school, I decided to write poems which is where *thoughts of a teenage girl* all began. I poured my heart, mind, and soul into these pages to finally express how I feel.

This is my dream. This is my life. This is *me*. Laid out before your very eyes. You will get to see parts of myself that people closest to me haven't noticed. Is it scary? Heck yeah! I can't help but wonder what you'll think of me after this. Will you think I'm crazy? Emotional? Girly? Awful? Dramatic? Relatable? Depressed?

Regardless of your opinions, (well, obviously I hope you like the book) take these words as a message from my heart. I feel so many different emotions every single day and forming them into words of poetry seems to be the only way I can control them. Some of these poems may be relatable, some you may understand, some you might stop and think, *what the heck does this have to do with anything?*

Well, just to remind you, these are my thoughts, my ideas, my feelings, and even some random scenarios that live in my mind day in and day out. Take with this book what you will, but I just want to say one last thing before you dive in.

You are currently looking, reading and holding one of my greatest dreams. Thank you for that.

katherine mazzei

thoughts of a teenage girl.

thoughts of a teenage girl.

girls from ages
thirteen to nineteen
all have weird thoughts
and different dreams.

some are so young,
so pure,
so innocent.

while others have been through it all
thick and thin.

an age of girls
who don't know where they belong.
too young to grow up,
yet too old to be a kid.

a fourteen-year-old could have
her life figured out
while an eighteen-year-old could
have
no clue what she's going to do
with her life.

thoughts of a teenage girl.

we are just girls
on the brink of adulthood,
trying to understand where we
belong
before it's too late.

because time moves fast
and the world won't slow down
for a bunch of teens
trying to fit in.

bad things will happen,
good things will happen,
and your thoughts will always be in
your mind.

as you grow up,
life begins to shift
from princess dresses
to ripped jeans
and you start to wonder
what your purpose is.

along with these wonders
come your thoughts
piling up within you
begging for answers.

so, in order to clear
my own thoughts,
i do what i know best.

write them down.

thoughts of a teenage girl.

katherine mazzei

society.

thoughts of a teenage girl.

Society, to me, is a social concept created from popular ideas, opinions, and morals which have manipulated the minds of the people for centuries. These concepts are ever changing, depending on the trends at the time, and as I get older and become acquainted with the world, I see the inner workings of society more often whether it is virtual or physical. I have my own dreams, my own beliefs, and my own ideas. What if my views don't see eye to eye with the rest of the world? And if my opinions don't fit into society's "expectations", will I ever get to where I want to go? Society is a spectacle of wonder, yet at the same time, a vision of terror. It secretly haunts the world day and night yet somehow, it's not often a fear admitted by most people. That's because society is all the world has ever known.

why must beautiful things die?

colors paint the leaves in the trees
just like a picture.
the breeze gently plucks the leaves
away from the branches
where they are carried
gracefully by the wind
and laid
gently on the ground.

a flower blooms in late spring
as pretty as it can be
the fragrance is pungent
and sweet enough to make you smile.

but once the leaves
turn colorless and brittle,
and flower petals
become dry and weak
the world is certain that it is dead
because it no longer acquires beauty.

but how can such a
beautiful thing die?
why would a beautiful thing ever die?

it's not just
the leaves and the flowers
that radiate an enchanting picture
for all eyes to see.

it's also the beauty of certain people
who shine like the sun,
yet easily fade away
as though they were nothing.

how come those
with the kindest souls
are destined to be taken away
from the world
in just a matter of seconds?

why are wonderful people
easily forgotten,
whereas horrid ones
remain remembered?

why are those who contain goodwill
plucked away like a speck of grass
when their purpose was to shock the
world with their tender affection?

these are the people
with the most beauty
which make the world brighter
just like the way leaves and flowers
construct an outdoor picturesque.

this leads to one last question
which i ponder in mind
simply, i must ask
why must beautiful things die?

let me be

questions?
too many questions
that i don't know the answers to.

time?
let it stand still for a while.
why am i always in a rush?

thoughts?
why so many?
and why do they constantly hurt?

just let me be.
let me be.
let me be.

i'm struggling enough as it is,
so quit piling more problems
on top of me.

please, oh, please
just let me be.

days?
they come faster that i can count.

nights?
are always lonely.

the future?
is a mystery to me.

when?
i don't know.

why?
i'm not sure.

how?
can you just stop!?

let me be!
let me be!

so many questions.
so many thoughts.
so little time.

can't i just live in the moment?
stay in a peaceful place?

maybe i can,
if only society would just let me be.

let me be.
let. me. be.

temptations

my friends are all at parties
while i'm just a good girl
sitting at home, reading.
but the temptations…

everyone seems to be in relationships
whereas i haven't even had
my first kiss
maybe i should try it…
the temptations…

go, get in your car.
who cares about the consequences?
they always get away with it…
the temptations…

the temptations
overwhelming, thoughtless
temptations
which swarm my mind.

are you a good girl for not doing it,
or are you a coward?

what if i just…
maybe if i…
will i feel alive?

oh, the temptations.

wasting my time

i hate it when i look at you
because i'm only wasting my time
and my life.

but it's hard to stop when
i'm addicted to you
because everyone is addicted too.

you're like a vampire, sucking blood
slowly killing me,
and draining my life away
with your sharp teeth.

you make me feel controlled.
every. single. time.
but still, i don't know what to do.
obviously, neither does anyone else.

when i'm bored,
i turn to you.

when i'm tired,
i turn to you.

when i'm busy,
i turn to you.

because you're the easiest distraction.
you're the addiction.
and i can't control it
even though i know
you are wasting my time.

out of control

i'm losing it.
i'm crazy.
i'm psychotic.
i'm out of control.

i take the hammer
and swing it as hard as i can
against my reflection
that constantly tells me
i'm not pretty.

i grab my phone
and throw it across the room
because it takes my life away
every second of every day.

i grab my test paper
that tells me i am a failure.
i strike the match
and the paper goes ablaze.

kerosene drips from
the cardboard boxes
that are neatly in a pile.
i drop the burning, worthless
document

and flames rise up
towards the night sky.

grabbing my notebook
a blank sheet is there.
i take a pencil
and write all of my
bad thoughts down.

i rip the paper in shreds
and feed the burning flame
which luminates the night.

i'm out of control
and it feels great
to finally get all of it out.

everything i hate,
i break.
i destroy.
i burn.

and now, i am satisfied.

i'm just a kid

sometimes i stop and wonder
how on earth i got here
so close to adulthood,
yet still attached to my childhood.

often i forget
i'm just a kid
being rushed into a life
i'm not ready for.

i watch the people around me,
some in relationships,
others even getting engaged,
while i've never romantically
held hands.

it's crazy for me to think
that i'm growing up
when i don't even know
what i'm going to do
or who i'm going to be.

can society give me a moment
to pause,
to breathe,
and be a kid?

it's exhausting
being bombarded with questions
about the future.

just because i'm almost there,
doesn't mean i am.

give me my last few years
because in all reality
i'm just a kid
whose heart is too young
to grow up just yet.

civil

why is everything
always so divided?

why do all these disagreements
turn into fights?

when did all the civility in society
get up and walk away?

it's always,
i'm right you're wrong,
rather than,
i understand your side.

everybody is all talk
when instead, we should be listening.

why can't we just be civil?
why are we all so full of hate?
why is it so hard
to explain what i mean?

it's impossible anymore
to have a civil discussion
between people
with contrasting opinions.

why is that?

people blame everything
on one side alone
when obviously,
both have their faults.

instead of solutions
they come up with excuses.

they'd rather be stubborn
than give in a little
in order to make a compromise.

can you tell me why
we all can't be civil?

respect each other's opinions,
try to be open minded,
so we can create a solution?

tell me,
is incivility the answer?
because personally
i think it'll be our downfall.

but why listen to me?
who am i to say anything?

thoughts of a teenage girl.

i'm just a kid
trying to be civil
except i'll be considered a minor
forming a worthless opinion.

why do people in society always have to
prove that they are good enough? you can't
just be a good person, you have to do this,
do that, and constantly please people in
order to get what you want and where you
want to go. it is exhausting and i don't want
that to be my life. i want to take control, and
live my life the way it is supposed to be
lived regarding my own personal standards,
not others.

the incomprehensible idea of society

everyone tells me not to care
but when i try to do that
i can't.

all i want to do
is quit wasting my time
on something that i hate.

but, unfortunately, that's not possible
because what about everyone else?
if i quit, then i'm letting them down.

yet, i'm letting myself down
by continuing this way.

i just want to pause,
pause everything
and figure out
how to get out of this mess.

all i'm doing right now
is wasting my time
and it's exhausting
because time is so precious.

what if i died tomorrow
how incomplete would my life be?

how come society expects me
to meet and care for everyone's needs
before my own?

i need to love myself.
i need to trust myself.
i need to escape and figure things out.

but i can't let anyone down
nor can i waste my time
caring about what they think of me.

so, what's the verdict?
do i spend my whole life selfless
or selfish?

do i let my true colors fly
or only show those which are
appropriate?

should i care
or not care?

oh, how silly of me.
i must care for others.

i must do what is best for society and
the world around me,
even if it brings pain to myself
because that is the right thing to do.

oh, but how i wish my kindness
could reflect on them
and come back to me.

yet, no matter how kind,
how caring,
how thoughtful you are,
society deals the cards.

and if you disagree…
then you're the one
with all the consequences.

talentless

i want to do so much
but i only get so far
before i give up.

i want to do something great,
but i feel so talentless.
always writing down my ideas
but they don't make any sense.

i try to give myself assurance
that i'll make progress over time,
but when compared to everyone else
i'm the last in line.

i hate feeling talentless
all the time.
making me worthless
with everything i write.

if only i had talent
then maybe i'd feel fine.

8%

statistically, 8% of people
achieve their dreams.
the rest just give up,
never living out their
greatest hopes and desires.

i don't want to be
a part of the majority
and i am tired of hearing
that i will be
because that's where most
people end up.

i want to be a part of the 8%
of those who have succeeded,
of those who have worked hard,
and made it where they strived to be.

yes, people tend to hate the 8%.
why?
because they have
what 92% of people don't.

being jealous is tempting.
constantly wondering,
why can't that be me?

well, it can be me.
i'll just have to work really
hard to get there.

oh, it's disappointing
that those not a part of that 8%
will let jealousy overcome them
leading to words of hate and disgust
towards those who don't deserve it.

i assure you, that won't be me.
because hateful words
will not make my dreams come true.

instead, i will focus on my goal
and see everyone on the other side
once i become a part of the 8%.

shut up, shut up, shut up!

it feels like everyone
is constantly telling me
that i'm wrong
and interrupting
all my thoughts.

it makes me mad.
it makes me sick.
you expect me to act like an adult,
yet treat me like a kid.

can't you let me say
what i have to say
instead of talking
over me?

if you actually
listened to my point
you'd realize
i'd prove to be right.

instead, you're all talk
and i'm silent
except in my mind
i'm screaming.

if only i could shout,
the words would be,
shut up, shut up, shut up!

what's the worst that could happen?

constantly i am afraid
of everything that i do
because if i mess up
my future comes to a halt.

but realistically,
what's the worst that could happen?

if i request a favor or ask a question
am i really that afraid
of the answer?

or if i wear a piece of clothing
that contrasts my regular wardrobe,
will anyone really care?

what's the worst that could happen
if i say what's on my mind
rather than stay quiet
all the time?

will they hate me
if so
who cares?
i will move on anyway
and live to see another day.

honestly, in this little world of mine
what's the worst that could happen?

don't belong

everybody is a piece
in a puzzle
and they are easily placed
without hesitation.

i try to fit my piece
into society's puzzle
but somehow,
i don't fit.

i adjust.
i change.
i move.
but still, i don't fit.

what if i became smaller?
would i fit in place then?

what if i changed?
would the puzzle
make room for me?

or would my attempts be useless
because i'm not destined to fit in?

it is so exhausting

trying to adjust to a world
which constantly shuts you out
and makes you feel worthless.

i'm tired of trying
to fit in society's puzzle
so maybe i don't belong.
and maybe
i never will.

my own worst enemy

i think about that
embarrassing moment
all the time,
and i hate myself
because it happened.

when i am asked to define myself
words form in my mind,
imperfect, stupid, spoiled,
ugly, disappointing.

why is it so easy
to point out the bad things,
yet so hard
to point out the good?

it's because
i'm my own worst enemy.

constantly, i think i can do better,
be better,
but i always expect
too much of myself.

i have all A's.
i should be proud of myself,
but instead i'm frustrated
because i don't have
the highest grade in the class.

what is the point of being happy,
when you're not the best?

instead of celebrating,
i keep pushing myself.

i lost a couple pounds,
but my jean size is still the same,
i still look the same,
so maybe, i need to try harder,
push myself even farther.

does it hurt?
yes, but i deserve it
because i am my own worst enemy.

i claim to love myself,
but that love is disguised as hate.
it's agonizing that i feel this way
because deep down,
i know i deserve better.

thoughts of a teenage girl.

i know that i'm a wonderful,
beautiful person,
inside and out,
i just never describe myself that way.

because it is so easy
to be selfless in society.
that's what you're supposed to be,
and maybe that's why
i am my own worst enemy.

manipulation

my whole life
i have been blinded
by the people i love
who claim they've made me strong,
yet i've only become weak.

my whole life
i have been told
to never date a boy.
never kiss a boy.
never love a boy.

and i have listened
because i give those i love
all my trust
and all my attention
to make them happy.

because of that promise
i secretly made to them
i have spent nights,
hours,
years,
wondering what would happen
when i finally did
break that promise.

by that time, i would still be
innocent,
vulnerable,
hopeful,
trusting,
loving,
just like i am now.

oh, but that doesn't mean
he will share the same characteristics.

i have been told
so many things
and what if
i get sucked into something
that was expected to be love,
but turned out to be torture?

the thought of my idea of love
being twisted into hurt
kills me.

so, how do you prepare
for the wounds
when you don't know how much
pain they will inflict on you?

i have been told
to be respectful,
to be polite,
and to be quiet.
i have done all those things.

even the temptations
aren't strong enough
to break the trance
which has been imprinted
into my brain,
into my heart,
and into my soul for years.

when my friends
make me mad,
sad,
or hurt,
i don't do anything.

why?

well, if i did
in the end, i would be
the only one standing
because friends come scarce and few
and i can't afford to lose them.

thoughts of a teenage girl.

society has pressed
this image of who i should be
in my thoughts.

and it has made me push
farther and harder.
yet the results have been pointless
and only harmful to my well-being.

how have i not been able
to notice it before?
how have i not noticed
the fact that society has been
manipulating me?

my strings have been exposed
my entire life
and people think it's okay
to constantly stretch them thin.

no wonder everyone is so proud.
i am exactly who they want me to be
a follower,
never a leader.

my confidence has been shot
and my self love barely exists.

i am so sick of it
and have been for a while,
but this has been my whole life.
how do i walk away from it now?

how do i let go of the rope
that others have told me
is the only connection
to happiness
even though
it is burning my hands?

how do i stand up
after being walked all over
for sixteen years?

how do i treat others
the way they are treating me
when my whole life
i have been kind?

my eyes are starting to see
what once was blind to me
and i cannot let the world
impair my vision any longer.

to make things clear
your little scheme
whether you intend it or not
is hurting me.

and if you really care about me,
stop constantly putting pressure
on everything that i do.

stop claiming that your
words of wisdom
are actually helping
because i am not you
and you are not me.

stop inserting yourself
into what decisions
are the best ones
that i will make.

your manipulation
is killing me.
just because it isn't physical
doesn't mean that there are no scars.

trust me,
deep down
i am thoroughly wounded
by your ignorant manipulation.

what is right and what is wrong?

life gives us a chance
to make mistakes,
to learn new things,
and to overcome obstacles.

society is a dynamic wonder
that shifts people's minds
into what is right
and what is wrong.

what was right a hundred years ago
can be very wrong today.

so i'm going to ask one thing:
what is right and what is wrong?

people interpret right and wrong
in many different ways.

there are different cultures
and beliefs
in which focus
on what is truly
good and evil.

but different people
live different lives.
therefore, their moral values
impact their definition of
right and wrong.

will people accept this
theory though?
or are people so set on
their own morals
that they shut out other ideas?

obviously, i have my own beliefs,
but how can the whole world
find the line in which divides
what is right and what is wrong
when there are so many people
who carry their own values?

it may be a silly question
but at the end of the day
it can be the silly questions
that create the most controversy
amongst a world
full of very different human beings.

education

educate yourself,
that's what i want to do,
but who and what
can i– should i believe anymore?

facts start to look like opinions
and opinions look like facts.
how am i supposed to understand the
difference between true and false?

i want to read books
that will answer my questions,
but unfortunately don't have time
because of a pile of homework
i have no interest in.

i want to be smart
i really do,
but every second i spend at school
feels like i'm losing any intelligence
i may have.

i failed the test that i studied for
so now a number,
a letter,
defines my worth.

i got the question wrong
even with my confident answer.
now, i feel stupid
and hide my face in shame.
all because i made a mistake.

i try to ask the question,
how will this help me
in the real world?
yet, i never get an answer.

when i bring up the point
that humans weren't made
to sit in a classroom
for seven hours a day
i am ignored.

i'm sixteen
i've just got my first taste
of the real world
and instantly wanted to take it back
because there is no way
i'll be ready for it all
by the time i graduate.

thoughts of a teenage girl.

so let me say thank you
to my current *education*
for doing nothing
but control what i do,
what i learn,
and who i'll end up being.

because after all these years
i'll constantly be dependent,
feel stupid,
and appear lost in the real world.

katherine mazzei

thoughts of a teenage girl.

doubt.

thoughts of a teenage girl.

Doubt is the lingering burden which weighs down any good idea that I have within myself, making it hard to believe those ideas are valuable and worth pursuing. It is a constant reminder that I am unsure about the future and what my purpose is. It has convinced me that my dreams are unattainable, and my work is never going to compare to others around me. Doubt is the root cause of my overthinking, and it leads to the exhaustion of my body. My own self-doubt tells me that I am not good enough for anything nor anybody in this world, and that no matter how hard I try, I will never be.

don't know who i am

i thought i had it all figured out.
i thought i knew who i was.
i stayed consistent for years
with the same hobbies,
but now, it's not the same.

i've tried to find my purpose
by looking up to those i admired,
but after years of doing that
i still haven't found myself.

i realize now that
i don't know who i am,
don't know where i belong,
and don't know how to find out.

i'm not a part
of a specific group of people,
and i don't know what i want to be
when i grow up
even though i'm almost there.

the cold, hard truth is
 i don't know who i am.

my whole life
decisions have been made for me,
but now i have to make my own.

it's scary growing up
not knowing where i will go next,
or failing to provide
 the correct answer
though what i feel people expect
from me
is perfection.

what if i make the wrong choice,
become someone that i am not,
and ruin my life forever?

what if i regret my life,
wish that i could take it back,
and change it all
but can't because it's too late?

how long will it take to know
who i am,
or will i never find out?

so many questions
and the only answer i have is
i don't know who i am.

two steps behind

everybody is moving along
at a fast and steady pace.
they have a goal,
they know what they're doing,
they know who they are,
but i don't.

i feel like i'm always
 two steps behind
tripping and stumbling
on my own two feet
trying so hard to keep up
with the crowd
but they are always ahead of me.

i have great dreams,
but who am i to achieve them?

who am i?
what am i?
where do i belong?
why am i taking forever to get there
while others are moving on?

just work harder, they say,
be faster and you'll be right there
with them.
still, it seems the harder i try
the slower i get.

no matter how much effort
i put forth towards my dreams,
i am always two steps behind
following others like a lost puppy
not knowing where i will go next.

you have potential, they begin,
you'll make it eventually,
yet how much hope can i hold?
how much patience can i test?

will i have enough time
to make it where i ought to be?
or will i be a failure
and lose sight of my dreams?

because no matter how hard i try
they are always in the lead
then there i am
two steps behind.

give up

nobody told me
that growing up would be so hard.
nobody told me
that i would feel so many emotions
that i can't explain.
nobody told me
that i would lose motivation
just in the simplest things.

when i put in effort,
i expect to gain something out of it,
but instead i fail
over and over again.
nobody told me that would happen.

every single day
i wonder, what would happen
if i gave up?
what would happen if i just stopped?
what if i no longer put in the effort?

my mind circles around those words,
give up.
give up.
give up.

and some days, it's tempting.
as though i'm on the cusp
of doing so.
like i'm on the edge of a cliff
so close to falling off.

somehow,
i manage to continue,
but the weight of the idea
is so heavy.

so so heavy.
those two simple words
which stay in my mind.
give up.
give up.
give up.

there she goes

there she goes
the little girl
everyone gave
so much hope in.

there she goes
falling down the stairs again
praying she can get up on her own
because no one will lend a hand.

there she goes
straight to her room
and sits all alone
drowning herself in a world
full of lost dreams and hopes.

oh.
there.
she.
goes.

she tells everyone around
that she's fine
but she's not.

they say fake it till you make it
yet so far, it hasn't worked for her.

there she goes
her childhood slipping away.
all she wants is a place to be
even though she's 17.

there she goes
crying again
because she doesn't fit in.

she isolates herself from the crowd
to avoid the awkward
interactions with others
because deep down
she knows she will never be *enough*
for rest of the world.

oh.
there.
she.
goes.

desperate

constantly,
i feel the need to dodge any
chance at romance
because i can't have it.

i'm afraid
that one day
i'll become desperate.

desperate for something
that'll mean nothing
in the long run.

how long can i wait
for my love
to come rescue me
from my loneliness?

will i become desperate
and blind myself
in order to feel
something?

and if i do, then will i realize
that it was nothing
and regret
that i didn't wait?

if you can read this somehow,
please
don't leave me here too much longer
because i don't want to be alone.

i don't want to be *desperate*.

but what if you don't exist?
and i'm never rescued?

my mind forms the doubts
and what if i am destined to be
desperate
because there is no one out there
who will love me?

good girl

she's a good girl
that's her reputation
spoken of so highly
she can barely face it.

everyone always talks about
how she's gonna do great things
in her life.

but in her mind
she always wonders
if their predictions
are right.

because what if they're wrong
and she fails them all?

she's a good girl
but her own worst enemy.
always striving to be perfect,
but constantly pointing out her flaws.

since she is a good girl,
she spent the whole night
silently crying
then woke up the next day smiling

because that's what the world expects
from her.

she's a good girl
with bad habits,
but she hides them
in the dark.

often,
she thinks about doing
bad things
so she can experience
breaking the rules for the first time,
yet her ideas fall through in real life.

she's overwhelmingly in the blue
but people think she's fine
so, of course, everything is alright.
except, it's not.

they're all too blind by her
generosity
to see her
true feelings of insecurity.

she's a good girl,
but boys don't love her.

a good girl,
yet all alone.

what if she'll never find
a crowd of her own?

well, for now
everything's all right
because the adults in her life
swear she's the perfect child.

such a good girl
with a sad mind
don't let it go to waste
and ruin your life.

stay humble,
stay kind.

she's a good girl.
such a good girl.
an amazing child.
they all call her
a good girl.

but secretly
she doubts
her title
is truly earned.

hidden

i've tried
again and again
to peek from the shadows
and reveal who i am.

i bring it all to the table
because my confidence is high
and my fear is low.

i put myself out there
just to see what it's like.

but none of them care.

none of them pay attention.

so, maybe it's better
if i keep myself hidden.

i know it's all in my head
but i can't help wondering:
why don't they like me, again?

it's like a scheme
they have against me.
i can watch the fun,
but never be included.

yet, when i get the guts
to ask about what they are up to,
all they do is
ignore me.
like i'm nothing.

i envy their fun.
i envy their love.
just why can't they let me in?

it's like they are giving me a chance
reeling me in their direction,
but every time i try to make
it to them
they let me go.

can you tell me
if it will always be like this?
because so far i've spent
much of my time
hidden.

thoughts of a teenage girl.

and i firmly believe
nobody will ever bother
to lurk in the shadows
in order to find me
because why step out of the
light,
when there is so much fear of the
dark?

pretty

my mom says that i'm pretty
and so does my family
but is it really true?

how come they are the only ones
who call me pretty?

i almost swear
that all the girls around me
are much better looking
than i am.

i get told that i look like my mom
and she's a beautiful woman
inside and out,
but i just don't see
her beauty in me when i need it
the most.

maybe it's hidden
beneath the layers and layers
of self-doubt,
and acts of putting myself down
in order to stay
humble.

thoughts of a teenage girl.

or maybe, i just can't see
from my perspective
the word *pretty*
being used to describe
me.

restless

my mind
won't let me be at peace
even though
i'm trying to sleep.

constant thoughts
run through my head
about how i'm lost
and always behind.

about how i'm lonely
and don't fit in.

about how i've never
been able to love,
yet all the people around me
are in relationships.

about the dreams
i haven't reached
and the exhausting self-doubt
that lingers and never goes away.

about the consistent *what ifs?*
and flashbacks of
embarrassing moments
i've experienced.

these are the thoughts
that keep me awake.

these are the thoughts
that keep me restless.

fake it till you make it

pretend to not care
so much about what other people
think of you
and eventually
you won't.

pretend to have confidence,
keep your head up,
and sooner or later
your confidence will be alive.

pretend to be fearless,
remind yourself,
what's the worst that could happen?
then you'll live your life
without fear.

pretend to love yourself,
be content with every part of you
inside and out,
and in time
you will love who you are.

you know what people say,
fake it till you make it,
unless, of course
you don't.

hush

the intrusive thoughts
that i try to push away
never go away,
and the pressure that they build
brings the fear that they will surface
and slip past my lips.

hush,
i remind myself,
don't let it slip,
you have a reputation.
what is my reputation exactly?
good girl, innocent, forgettable?

i don't let the words
slip from my lips
but in my mind
they are used constantly.

does that make it a sin?
or is it okay
since nobody knows?

i am the only one
who truly knows myself,
and the only one who knows
how dark i can be
underneath the sunshine personality i
am perceived
to obtain.

part of me wants to prance,
and prove everyone's idea
of who i am
to be wrong.

sometimes,
i want to risk it all
rather than always
focus on the consequences.

oh, hush now!
you can't do that!

i know.
i know.
everyday, i remind myself to think
before i speak.

oh, but how nice it would be
to say what was on my mind
and not care
about how i would be perceived.

the girl who seeks to be seen

she's always behind the camera.
always behind the scenes.
always catching a glimpse
of others living out their dreams.

but when will it be her turn?

if she is already
lurking in the shadows
at seventeen,
then where will she be
at forty-three?

where time has only moved forward,
she's only gotten older,
and her beauty begins to shift
into a face of constant fear
that nobody will want to see.

will there ever be a time
where it's safe to come out?
to completely be herself
without the judgment of others?

or will she always be at the bottom
stuck below those she
wanted to walk with?

no matter where she ends up
in her years to come
she vows to herself
that she will tend to those
in her position right now.

because not only does she want to
live out her greatest dreams,
she wants to help others
achieve theirs as well
rather than judge them
for where they are
in the beginning.

but in the back of her mind
she wonders if she'll
ever get herself unstuck,
or if all her dreams
are just false hopes
too good to be conquered
by someone behind the scenes.

thoughts of a teenage girl.

pain.

thoughts of a teenage girl.

Pain in many forms has one thing in common: it hurts. Much of the root cause of my pain comes from my heart, struggling to bear the horrible thoughts and ideas within myself. Pain can grow from just scenarios that I create in the middle of the night or a conversation I had with someone that ended in a fight. It hurts and it hurts so much to the point where I am frustrated and disappointed with myself because in the end, I am the problem. It hurts even worse when you realize that all this pain is targeted towards that little girl who used to sing on stage and wear princess dresses. Sometimes I wonder, how did I end up feeling so much pain in such little time?

falling under

my mind is trapped
in a void of darkness,
the more i try to escape,
the more i feel pain.
the chance to leave lost forever,
so now i'm just falling under.

my breathing gets shallow
and my eyes are glued
to my reflection.

i see my pale face,
with tears falling down my cheeks,
and wonder how
i made it to this point.

i can feel my heart and soul
crack like ice
and i pray i can piece
everything back together,
but my hands only shake,
and it's impossible to mend.
what has already fallen apart.

the void suddenly shines
a bright light
and my sobs grow louder.
fear has shattered
the pieces of my heart
and my mind knows that it's all over.

gullible

my eyes see someone in need.
my heart trusts that i should help.
my mind delays in its thinking.
i've been caught in a trap.

all because i was kind.

all because i was blind.

easily deceived i am.
easily manipulated.
they take advantage of a nice girl
because they don't feel any guilt.

why not benefit from
someone's sweet character?
why not take advantage
of those who love others?
why not make them feel small?
why not make them hurt?

then, once the person i trusted
deceives me,
i blame myself
because i should have seen it coming.

but, how could have i known?

i guess i always see the best in people
especially those who do
the most harm to me
because i'm a gullible little girl
who is now starting to see
the real world.

and to be completely honest,
i'm not sure i'll make it there.

spoiled girl

spoiled girl how ungrateful you are.
how can you be unhappy?

spoiled girl go get a job,
so that you can
earn your own money.

spoiled girl go touch some grass.
you need to do something productive.

spoiled girl how can you
go on like this
without a care in the world?

look at you, getting what you want
without even asking.
how can you say that life is hard
when you are given plenty?

oh, you thank them.
oh, you are grateful.
then why don't you show it more?

why are you lazy?
why are you privileged?
why are you even here?

you spoiled, spoiled girl
don't deserve anything in this world
when you do nothing good for it.

oh, but you say you try?
you say you want to?
then what's holding you back?

why can't you give the world more?
why can't you be perfect all the time?
why do you always get
what you want,
yet still feel bad about yourself?

shall you be punished?
would that make you better?
who is there to punish you
but yourself?

maybe you are let off too easily
by others,
so let yourself do the job.

go look in the mirror
and list off all the things
about how imperfect you are

now, you can be punished
with the hurt you deserve
to feel.

cry yourself to sleep at night,
feel hopeless and weak,
because you are a spoiled girl
who's her own worst enemy.

spoiled,
spoiled,
spoiled girl.

you shouldn't be surprised
that you're not good enough
for this world.

sometimes, i think of those
who i love the most dying.
and that's scary.

don't go

no.
no.
no.
stop, please don't go.

i don't want you to leave me,
forever
and ever
i love you too much.

i'd miss you constantly.
promise me you'll never leave me,
please?
please!
don't go.
don't go!

why do i think of you dying
late at night
while you're asleep in the next room?

i scare myself with my thoughts
of the ones i love most
leaving me forever.

even when i try to tell myself
that it will never happen
i still cry,
cry,
cry.

because the thought
of never seeing you again
hurts so bad.
promise me
that you will never leave me?
please don't go.
god, please
don't take them away from me
too soon.

please,
don't go.
don't go!

disappointment

i don't want to do it anymore, i'll say.
what do you mean? they'll reply.
i will repeat myself,
and silence will be the only sound.

i'll watch the disappointment
fill up in their eyes
while mine are full of tears.

i wish it were different, i'll begin.
i wish i can pretend
but the longer i go on
the more hurt i am.

they won't say anything back,
and i'll walk away.

i'd officially give up something
that people love me the most for
and they'll be disappointed.

it began when over the years
i started to realize
that i wasn't the girl
i thought i was.

if i tell them how i feel,
the conversations will stir.
she had so much potential,
they'll say,
too bad she threw it all away.

i will repeat over and over,
i'm so sorry.
i'm so sorry.
i'm so sorry.

but will it ever be enough?
will the apologies take
back what i did?
will the apologies change
my own mind?

no.
no, because i've changed.
my heart has changed.
my dreams have changed.

but i'm not sure
others will see it that way.

instead, from their perspective,
i'll be the girl
who went from her family's
biggest pride,
to their
shocking disappointment.

hurt

roses are red
violets are blue
everything you said
breaks me in two.

telling me i'm not enough,
making me feel useless.
you say that i should be tough,
but don't explain how
i can get through this.

everything within me is full of hurt,
inside and out,
and i'm lying in the dirt
surrounded by self-doubt.

because everything i feel
is filtered in shades of blue
which makes it hard to heal,
and now i don't know what to do.

pain and i,
we are the same.
no matter how hard i try
i can't change that claim.

thoughts of a teenage girl.

hurt is all i feel anymore,
and it's like a sin,
constantly fighting this endless war
where no one ever wins.

don't grow up little girl

everyone warns you not to grow up,
but i know you won't listen
because you envy those
older than you.

i understand.
i did too.

now that i'm older,
the world has shown me
its true colors.

i watch you,
only a little younger than me,
and feel pity
because i know
what will happen next.

this world doesn't deserve
to take away the innocence
of little girls like you,
but one day it will
and i can't do anything about it.

thoughts of a teenage girl.

this world doesn't deserve
to take away your happiness,
and make you feel
worthless.

little girl,
you don't hate yourself, do you?
of course not!
you shouldn't.

but the world will change you,
and make you feel that anger
towards yourself.

instead of loving your body
just the way it is,
you'll be told
it's not good enough.

you'll be told that you're
too annoying,
or that you talk
too much.
so, you'll shut up
and keep quiet,
slowly losing yourself in the process.

i know you don't understand,
and i don't have the heart to tell you
face to face.
but little girl,
don't grow up
because this world
doesn't deserve to take you away.

childhood wonders

i cried again today
because it made me feel raw and real.

i cried about
the birds that stopped chirping,
and the colors that were fading.

i cried about
the past that's no longer present,
and the future
which is unknown.

tears fall down my face
and land on my pillow,
late at night
as i look back on my memories.

my heart begs to feel
the childhood wonders
that i try to remember.
but as i grow up,
they drift farther away.

come back! i yell.
make me happy again!
make me love myself!
make me carefree!
but my wishes are lost
in the childhood wonders
that linger in my heart.

notice me

hey,
what if i was gone,
would you notice?

what if i disappeared,
would you miss me?

what if i was hurt,
would you care?

and after that,
what if i came back?

would you notice me then?
after all the trouble i caused?
after all the pain i endured?

how many times do i have
to punch myself
in order for you to see the bruises?

how many times do i have
to stand on the edge
before you see that i'm about to fall?

how many times do i have
to try and make you notice me
before i push myself too far,
never to be seen again?

selfish

i am unhappy
for no good reason
at all.

i am not okay
which is stupid
because i should be.

look at all these people
going through hard times
and i'm here complaining
about my perfect little life.

i'm selfish,
and i hate myself for it.

melancholy

a tear falls
but i don't know why
and everything around
turns black and white.

song lyrics
begin to feel real
and all of my thoughts
are tangled up in webs.

good memories
start to fade away,
and the brightest parts of life
have faded into darkness.

laughter
turns into sobs,
and love
becomes hate.

happiness
turns into a depressive state
and optimism
becomes melancholy,

the meaning of life
doesn't align
with what i thought it was
when i was a kid.

just when exactly
will all of this pain
come to an end?

never good enough

flaws leak out
of everything that i touch.

all the sticky notes
on the wall
are supposed to be motivating words,
but all i see are lies.

every time I do something,
it's never good enough.
there is always something to fix,
something to correct.

all the time it is a competition.
there is someone better than me.
therefore, i am always the loser.

i studied the night before,
thought i knew it all,
but my grade said otherwise.

and the one who didn't study
got the perfect grade
and will get perfect grades
every. single. time.

never ever have i been good enough.
for myself.
for others.
for anyone.

though i put in the work,
put in the effort,
put in the time,
it is never enough.
therefore,
i am *never* going to be *good enough.*

bigger person

for weeks and weeks now
i've asked for your help
because you were supposed
to be my guide.

yet, you failed to do it
for the longest time
and i let it slide.

i've showed you the hard work
that i've put in
and you say
that it's weak.

then continue to change
everything
without an explanation.

you tell me
the night before
that i did *nothing*
and you did *everything.*

well, i tried, okay?

i really, *really*, tried hard to make it
the best it could be.
and now i'm sitting here
crying
like a little kid
because i didn't do *enough* for you.

oh, the urge to talk back.
the urge to yell, scream, and shout,
tell you that i've done the work
and how i practically begged
you to help me
in the first place—

but instead, i took a deep breath,
ignored the petty comments,
and did what i had to do.

because i knew
that being the bigger person
would be worth it in the long run,
and that all of your remarks
were worth none of my time.

though you hurt me,
i chose not to hurt you.
instead, i let it roll off my back,
and pretend nothing happened
because i am the bigger person.

friends

i joke around a lot
that i don't have friends
because
that's the truth, right?

yeah, people laugh at me for it,
i even laugh along with them,
but on the inside
it's not funny.

maybe if i keep joking around
you'll think i'm actually an
interesting person,
and want to be friends with me.

because every smile you make
is a step closer to friendship
even if getting there means
hurting myself in the process

though i often isolate myself,
i really do want friends
and i silently envy those
who have them.

i just hate being lonely
and friendless.
it makes me feel awful.

i wish i could somehow show you
how i feel
then maybe you would understand
why often i silently wish
that i could have some friends.

enduring

pain.
oh, how it hurts
like you're being stabbed
over and over
in the same spot.

it's within me
and i can't control
when it comes
or when it goes.

who knows how long
it will be with me?

it constantly reminds me
that i'm not okay
even though
i thought i already healed.

it makes me want to
tuck myself away
and hide from the world around me.

it makes me feel lonely,
angry,
sad,
confused.

this pain is like no other
this pain is enduring,
and i fear that i will
never find the cure
in order to be healed.

help

help!
i need help!
i'm screaming,
i'm shouting,
but it only results
in silence.

look me in the eyes,
please,
look at me and understand
what i need.

i've realized that this is a problem
that i can't fix on my own.

please help me.
please.
please…
please!!

ugly

often, i want to cover myself up
because of all the flaws
i see in the mirror.

insecurities revolve all around me,
making me self-conscious.
every second.
every day.

and when i am exposed,
all alone,
i look at myself
in disgust.

i shouldn't look like this.
shouldn't i look better?
i mean, i'm young
i don't like what i see,
so how will i ever be content
with my image when i'm older?

how come everyone else
looks so much better
than i do?

thoughts of a teenage girl.

i try to tell myself,
that i am healthy
but why don't i feel it
when i see myself look like this?

i don't starve,
but strive to work away
all the faults i see.

no results are shown.
the only thing i notice
are the aching pains
all over my body.

oh and that poor little girl
i used to be
is crying
since i lost so much of her
over the years.

that little girl was pretty,
and she had no doubt that she was.

now i look in the mirror
and the first word that comes to mind
is ugly.

katherine mazzei

thoughts of a teenage girl.

pain doesn't always grow from the words
and actions of others, sometimes it comes
from the deepest, darkest thoughts within
yourself. pain can be fear and my fear is that
no one will ever love me. instead, i will fall
again and again only to realize that my
innocence has been stripped away from me,
and my heart has been wounded by the lack
of love and trust. what if i get hurt? what if
i'm not good enough? what if i end up with
the wrong person? what if…

vulnerable

i was vulnerable,
breakable,
touchable,
but you didn't seem to mind.

you took my heart and soul
and kept it in your control
while i smiled as i looked
into your eyes.

at the time
i thought everything was fine
having your hand in mine
until i realized you never loved me.

i stopped as it hit me,
grabbed my chest,
and felt my heart drop.

then you let go of my hand,
had a smirk on your face,
and walked away from me
like you planned it
all along.

i dropped to my knees,
sobbing,
wishing i could dissolve
into the earth
and never be seen again.

oh how horrible you were
to break my fragile, vulnerable heart,
now impossible to put back together.

i let my guard down,
i trusted you,
only to be deceived by
your charming smile.

all of this heartbreak
because i was vulnerable.

a poem from *his* perspective

innocent girl

innocent girl, don't go telling lies
about you and me.

you loved what i did
and now you hate me.

don't say that i hurt you
because i never did
you only hurt yourself.

i knew you were innocent
we all did
but you were unapproachable,
yet i was tempted.

i walked up to you
and complemented your eyes,
you blushed.
that's all it took
for you to become mine.

every day i would do the same thing,
your cheeks would glow.
i noticed you started putting on
makeup,
and wearing better clothes.

i finally asked you out
and you said yes.

you signed a contract
and you never looked back.

therefore, you were mine.
all mine.

don't say that i stabbed you
in the back
because i never did
you stabbed yourself.

you wanted to be loved didn't you?
and i gave my love to you
all of it.
and now i'm the bad guy?

you did what i told you
and always said you were fine.
i don't see anything wrong with
how much love i showed you.

i taught you that there was
more to life
than everything being pretty.
i showed you the real world
and now you hate me.

well that's fine
and i don't need you
so i'll say goodbye,
but just realize
you put this on yourself.

you are the reason for our problems.

i gave you a chance
that you never deserved.

i shouldn't have to apologize to you
for my time being wasted
on a stupid, innocent, clueless, girl
who should have known better.

but didn't.

a poem from *her* perspective.

you ruined me

i was innocent
so so innocent
and you ruined it.

i liked the way your mouth moved
and showered me with compliments.
you were the first boy to tell me
that i was pretty
and i really thought you liked me—
loved me,
but i realized, you didn't.

you blinded me with your blue eyes
that looked into mine
while your hands were on my back
twisting the knife.

when you kissed me, i thought
it was true.
i thought it was love.
i thought it was you.

then we moved too fast
and i thought it was fine
even though it hurt
every single time.

i kept asking myself,
is this really love?

and then i asked you
and you said it was.

i believed you,
i really believed you.

even through the screams,
even through the pain,
i still loved you.

because i didn't know better.

now i can never go back
to the girl i was before you
because you ruined me,
inside and out.

you didn't just break my heart,
you shattered it.

you didn't just make me yell,
you made me scream.

you didn't just make me cry,
you made me sob.

you killed the innocence in me.
you murdered my idea of love.
you ruined me.

you let me go

the storm hit you hard,
you fell down
and couldn't get up,
but i took your hand
and helped you get back on your feet.

i asked, *do you want me to let go?*
you said, *no*
so i didn't.
instead, i held you close.

it was so hard for you
considering the cards you were dealt,
but i had a pretty good deal,
so i gave you some of
my cards to play.

you seemed thankful,
at least you did in my eyes,
so i was happy
to give you parts of me
in order to heal parts of you.

i tried to love your pain away.
i healed your scars with my touch
and you ignited my heart
with your lips.

then everything within me shattered.
i thought i lost it all
but then i realized, i had you.

you could put me back together
just like i did with you.
you could heal my pain
and i believed it.

i looked at our hands
that weren't holding anymore.
i forgot we let go,
a little while back.

so i grabbed it again
like i needed your touch
to keep me alive,
looked into your eyes,
and prayed you could
see my urgency.

but you didn't.

thoughts of a teenage girl.

your eyes were emotionless,
loveless,
and i didn't know what to do.

you looked away
and i tried not to feel hurt
but i did.

i spent a moment
thinking it over
not wanting to ask
because i was afraid of the answer.

finally, i said it
are you letting me go?
you nodded.

my worst fear came true.
you let me go.

crushed

there is a boy
i have a crush on.
i've liked him
for six months now.

school is about to end
and i gain the courage
to ask him
if he likes me back.

my heart is racing.
my eyes follow his path.
i shout his name,
but he doesn't hear me.

i start to sprint,
try to get to him before he's gone.
once i catch up, i tap on his shoulder.
he turns around.

hey, i start
oh, hi, he replies.
i wanted to ask you something.
sure..., he continued,
um, what's your name again?

thoughts of a teenage girl.

oh, he doesn't know my name.

i tell him my name.
my heart starts to sink.

i just wanted to ask…
can you hurry up? he interrupted,
i'm in a rush

oh, um… nevermind, i say.
he rolls his eyes and walks away.

he, who was once my crush
has left me crushed.

one-sided love

i observe you from afar
and you are just…
gorgeous.

but you will never know
how perfect you are
in my mind.

i don't know why i feel
the way that i do
but what i do know
is that i can't stop thinking about you.

of course
i have to realize
that this is a one-sided love
and you probably don't
think about me
at all.

oh no.
this is going to hurt.

why can't my heart
stop falling for those
who will never care?

gosh, but you are such a gentlemen
you light up every room
that you walk in
and i see that.

but you don't see me.

and i know you will never feel as i do
but…
maybe you'll change your mind.

eventually, that hope will dissolve
into a puddle of lost desire
where i will drown
in my own pity
because my heart was never yours
to break.

love isn't

love isn't the bruises on my body.
love isn't the tears that i've shed.
love isn't the mistake you've made
again and again.

if i can't trust you,
then are you really my lover?
sneaking girls in our home
the whole entire summer.
threatening me
every time that i talk back.

i know love isn't that.

love isn't being scared
instead of thrilled
when you walk through the door.

love isn't praying that i can
escape someday.

love isn't stealing all my
hopes and dreams away.

how can you love me when i'm
deprived of it?

thoughts of a teenage girl.

you say that you love me,
but only after you hurt me.

you've manipulated me too long,
and i've nearly died from it.

love isn't the relationship between
you and me.
and now i know that it will never be.

katherine mazzei

thoughts of a teenage girl.

katherine mazzei

dreams.

thoughts of a teenage girl.

Dreams are my secret hopes and desires which replay in my mind, not only in my sleep, but as I am awake. My dreams come in many forms. Whether it is the idea of love or simply wanting a friend, I hold my dreams in a special place in my heart. But the real question is, will my dreams come true? Will I find the love of my life? Will I become a bestselling author? Will I live my life to the fullest? Will all of those silly fantasies I think about become a reality?

what if?

what if i fall?
i'll pick you up.

what if i break?
i'll put you back together.

what if i cry?
i'll dry your tears.

what if i'm lost?
i'll find you.

what if i fail?
i'll help you succeed.

what if i hurt?
i'll help you heal.

what if we go our separate ways?
i'll make my way back to you.

what if you hate me?
i could never hate you.

what if you love me?
then the truth would finally be told.

go

i'm sitting still
listening to the lyrics fill my head,
the beat of the music,
rushing my adrenaline.

i can no longer be still.

my leg shakes the table.
my thumbs rub together.
i can barely sit here any longer.
all i want to do is go.

i want to jump up and run,
run as fast as i can
and never stop.

i want the music in my ears,
the wind in my hair,
and my legs pushing off the ground
as i sprint.

all i want to do is go.
go.
go.
go.

thoughts of a teenage girl.

to go and never stop.
to sit still no longer.
will someone let me out of this trance
and set me free?

lead me to the place
where i want to be
for i will go go go
and be happy for eternity.

right now, nobody knows my name. don't
worry, you'll see it in lights someday.

i'm gonna prove you wrong

i'm gonna prove you wrong.
i'm gonna leave my mark
and it will be strong.

you'll regret what you said,
you'll regret what you did,
and what you didn't do

i'm gonna stand tall,
work hard,
and someday,
i'll be ahead of them all
even if now i seem so far behind.

i will work
night and day
i don't care how long
it will take.

years.
months.
weeks.
days.
it doesn't matter.

i know i am going to do something
that's going to shock the whole world
especially *you.*

so, if you don't mind
to leave me be.
i'll show you just what i can do.

i may lose the battles in the
beginning,
but the tides will turn
and my name will be shining under
victory.

you think it's impossible now
but when you see my name shining in
lights
you'll be staring in disbelief.
too bad at that point,
i'll already forget your name.

so, act as you do now
i'll be okay.
just remember these words
i'm gonna prove you wrong.

world of ink

how hard would it be
to let me live in a world of ink?
where the pages are full of stories
that i fantasize happening in my life.

people will tell me
that it's just a world of ink
nothing to get excited about,
but it's so much more than that.

it's an escape
from the real world
which is suffocating my happiness.

fiction lets me breathe.
fiction makes me feel alive.

it gives me hope
that i can find happiness,
find *the* one who i will spend
the rest of my life with.

maybe you think it's silly
that i spend my time reading books
but they contain words which hold
much power,
more than you think.

but you can continue your daily life
living in the real world
thinking that books are a
waste of time.

i'll just continue living
in both worlds.
one with you,
and one in a world of ink.

thoughts of a teenage girl.

would you, could you?

could you take a second
to look at me
and tell me that i'm pretty,
so i can believe it myself?

would you take a moment
to get to know me
and be my friend,
giving me something special?

if our hearts traded places,
could you carry the weight
of my heart?

would you let me feel
your love,
your dreams,
your hopes, and desires?

could you be trustworthy,
loving, and kind
without stabbing me in the back?

i will do everything to take care of
your heart
make sure it is protected
with *my* love and *my* trust.

but…

would you, could you
do the same?

visions

we are sitting outside on
our front porch
listening to old records
because those are the best.

it's beautiful outside,
the perfect temperature.
we are looking towards the fields
which stretch for miles and miles.

it is perfect.

we look back on the memories
that we had together
and hold hands
like we have for years.

all of it is perfect
but it's just a vision.

**

i looked at you and the
world stopped turning.

177

i can't believe we are here today.
your eyes are full of tears
but you're not in pain.

you took my hand
and placed it in yours.
we said our vows,
so well written we were both in tears.
my heart was racing and i said *i do*
then we kissed.

but it's all just visions.

because right now i'm in my room
trying to write a love story,
but i don't know where to begin.

i've never been in love
but is it hard to envision it?

or are my visions
just a source of delusion?

attention

she gets all the attention
from all of her friends
and even those who don't know her
look across the room in wonder.

i envy her sometimes
even though she's not my friend
but just to have people notice you
seems like a dream.

i try to show who i am
to the people around me
but it fails, miserably
when compared to her.

the fear of harsh opinions
leaves me lurking in the shadows,
observing those around me
who are so happy.

i want that attention.
i want to be seen.
i want to be heard.

yet, why am i always invisible?
why am i always quiet?

i really want some attention
except, i fear the opinions of others
tearing me apart.

maybe if i do something great,
i will get a glance from them all.

but for now

i will only be an observer
rather than the girl
who gets all the glory,
all the love,
all the attention.

nights in the city

the glowing lights.
the cool clear air.
windows rolled down.
wind in my hair.

the music playing loud
for all of us to hear
and the large buildings
that tower over us.

it's these nights in the city
which feel like you're in a fantasy
and luminate the whole world
with colorful light.

it's these nights in the city
where i feel like i'm on
another planet
and have no responsibilities.

it's these nights in the city
that make me feel alive,
adrenaline rushing through my veins,
lasting all night.

i love these nights in the city
because it brings together
both darkness and light.

i want it

have you ever been in love?
because i haven't.

yet can you just imagine
finding the one
who will care for you,
hold you,
love you?

you find someone
that looks at you
like you are the only girl
in the world.

he holds your hand,
opens the door for you,
kisses your lips,
and has the softest touch.

it is just so beautiful to me,
and i want it.
i really want it.

dear little me

dear little me,
how do you stay as happy
as you can be?
could you share a little
piece of happiness
with the girl you'll grow up to be?

dear little girl,
can we switch places
for just one day,
so that i can go play
with all of my old friends
before we went our separate ways?

hey little me,
how about you tell me
all the things you know about
who you are going to be?

oh, a beautiful princess?
that sounds nice
i really wish
i could make up my mind.

thoughts of a teenage girl.

well little me,
can you teach me
how to love
who i am?

you love yourself
i know this to be true
because you have nothing
to be ashamed of
but unfortunately, i do.

little me
you sing so nice,
and you can do it in front of everyone
without a hint of fear.

would it hurt you
if i told you
we don't do that anymore?

when you grow up
life can be a lot darker
than the sunshine and rainbows
that you are used to.

usually,
it's the younger ones
who ask those older than them
for advice.

but i can't help
asking little me
for guidance
because she managed to see
so much beauty
in the world around her.

dear little me
can you help
dry my tears
and bring back my smile?

dear little me
one last thing
i really miss you
and wish i could go back
and be your age again.

but i can't,
so for now, i'll be here.

thoughts of a teenage girl.

i miss you.
love,
your older self.

gone girl

gone girl
don't hesitate
run like the wind
and never look back.

the road you'll take
is gonna be long,
but in the end
you'll find your way home.

gone girl
get out of that bed
and go make yourself
a better life instead.

listen to me
it's okay to be afraid
as long as you've got courage
you're gonna do great.

quit hurting yourself
to make everyone feel okay
it's only bringing you down,
sinking your hopes and dreams away.

don't just follow your dreams,
catch them
because the longer they lead you on
the farther away you'll get.

gone girl,
make yourself anew
take some time
to focus on you.

it's gonna be hard
it's gonna be tough,
but your determination
will guide you through the rough.

so gone girl
don't you dare give up
because the work you put in
will take you beyond and above.

live in the moment

the shining golden sun
with rays that stretch
for miles around.
the fall leaves
drifting through the wind.

mountains tall,
full of colors
spreading out
for miles and miles.

life is full of beauty
we often overlook.

like the fresh air
we breathe in every day.
i am grateful for every breath
that i take.

like the sunrises in the morning
and the sunsets in the evening.
will we only take a picture,
or will we actually
live in the moment?

thoughts of a teenage girl.

take some time
and close your eyes,
so you can capture these memories
before they drift away.

breathe in.
breathe out.
smile.
laugh.

live in the moment
before it's lost.

live in the moment
while it lasts.

can we be friends?

for a while i've been looking
for someone who
could keep me company,
someone who could be my friend.

you caught my eye
and i couldn't help but wonder
just what it would be like
if i got the courage to say hi.

but how do you go up
and ask someone
if they want to be your friend?

because the fear of rejection
lingers on and on
inside my head.

but you just seem so nice,
so fun,
so passionate.

i can't help but smile
and wonder
if you were my friend,
how different would life be?

would it be brighter?
full of laughter and fun?
because from what i can see
you are *amazing*.

i guess the real question is
can we be friends?

falling in love with love

the beauty
of a boy
meeting a girl
in new york city.

they are worst enemies
or so they say
until they fall head over heels
for one another.

the sight
of watching a gentleman
look at a lady
in a drop-dead gorgeous dress
walk down the stairwell
raises every girl's expectations.

the lady blushes
and she looks back at the gentleman
feeling like the luckiest girl
in the world.

a book
that is full of beautiful words
contains dialog full of
love and affection
to describe how the main characters
feel about each other.

it makes you smile.
it makes your heart flutter,
your cheeks crimson,
and makes you realize…

you're falling in love with love
and you can't escape
the hopeless romantic dreams
you will forever have and associate
with the word *love*.

bittersweet

the idea of love
it's so bittersweet
because the term *love*
seems so
passionate, infinite, longing.

but sometimes, love can hurt.

the one you thought
you were going to marry,
ends up breaking your heart.

the boy you've loved for years,
doesn't even remember your name.

the guy you thought was yours
drops your hand
and expects you
to let him pick it right back up.

when love is shattered,
you wonder if you'll ever
feel it again
and it's terrifying
because what if you don't?

but just when you think
all hope is lost,
you find *the one*.

the one who doesn't even compare
to the others
because that is the real
love of your life.

but love itself
will never be defined the same way
as you first thought it would be.
from now on, the term, *love*,
is bittersweet.

him

i lay in the dark
unable to sleep
because i can only think
of the one thing i want.

i want *him.*

i want to feel *him*
right there beside me
his strong arms
wrapped around my waist
holding me close.

i want to feel *his* warm breath
against my skin
aware of *his* presence
that will keep me safe.

i want to feel the love
that radiates within *him*
making my heart ignite
an eternal flame.

thoughts of a teenage girl.

yet i can't feel *him*
when *he's* not there
because *he* is not in my life yet,
and one of my worst fears
is that *he* will cease to exist.

but i know for certain
he will always exist in my dreams.

desire

i crave attention
and i secretly wish
someone would care to ask
how i feel.

and when they ask me that question
i'll say that *i'm fine*, of course
but then, i want them to firmly state
what is true-

no, you are not fine-

rather than give themselves
brownie points
for at least asking.

i want to pour it all out
right in front of them
give them every little piece of me
without the fear of losing them.

i want a good friend
a really good friend
that i can relate to
and will put me before
all of their other friends.

thoughts of a teenage girl.

i want to be loved
like i've never been loved before.

i want to succeed
and have no regrets
in my life.

i want to be happy
and crossover that barrier
that keeps me away from happiness.

i have laid before you
my greatest desires.

maybe i am being selfish
maybe i am asking for too much
but i can't lie
about what i truly want for myself.
about what i truly desire.

innocent crush

we were just little kids
but we were the best of friends
i will never forget that.

i had known you for a while,
but then i started thinking
about *you*
more often.

drawing hearts around your name
it felt like some sort of dream.

it's all a little fuzzy
whether you actually asked me
if i *liked you*
and i lied by saying *no.*

or the time i chased you
and pecked my lips
against your cheek.

i can't remember if it was
actually real
or just my imagination.

thoughts of a teenage girl.

innocent crush,

you're the closest thing i've ever had
to love
and i don't even truly know
what love is.

i still think about you
even though i doubt you
remember my name.

i just find it comforting
to have the idea
of my innocent crush
coming back to me
all grown up
and falling in love.

just like the books
just like the movies
but so far
it's only been a thought within
my silly fantasies.

girlhood

i have always believed
that being a teenage girl
would make life enchanting.

i'd have a group of friends
who i would hang out with
constantly.

we'd go to the mall,
sleepover at each other's houses,
talk about boys,
and give each other makeovers.

we'd constantly beg
the first one who got her license
to take us places.

then we'd all have our license
and have the occasional
girl's night out
going to restaurants
laughing and giggling
about the most random things.

thoughts of a teenage girl.

then we would all spend weeks
planning out what we'd wear
to the dance,
pick out our dresses,
and meet up to get ready.

we'd cry about our break-ups
and gush over our crushes.
complain about our grades
and laugh at each other's jokes.

i guess that was my idea of the
teenage girlhood
i've wanted my entire life.

sadly, that's not how my girlhood
turned out to be.

dreamcatcher

the fear of not achieving my dreams
haunts me constantly
but with each word i write
i am one step closer to
conquering my fears.

this book may not make it far,
yet maybe it will.
either way, i am proud.

because i am embracing the process
in which i am writing this book
and slowly understanding
parts of who i am
within it.

will it prove that i can do it?
will it be the beginning of a journey
that i have been longing for my
whole life?

time can only answer my questions,
but for now, i will overcome the
lingering thoughts
of not chasing my dreams.

because right now
i am sprinting towards them,
and i don't plan to slow down
anytime soon.

katherine mazzei

thoughts of a teenage girl.

reality.

thoughts of a teenage girl.

Reality is exactly what it sounds like: my real life. It's not all sunshine and rainbows. It's not all pain and misery. It's just normal. The normal reality of a teenage girl who feels unsure, sad, happy, and confused all at once. It's the desire to go chase your dreams, yet the confinement of responsibilities holding you back. It's filled with the days where you want to curl up and bawl your eyes out, yet also filled with days where you want to dance, sing and laugh. Reality is when you feel so much love towards yourself, yet also so much hate. Reality is ever-changing, you never know what's going to happen next.

i'm okay

are you OK? they ask.
they've noticed my expression.
i'm okay, i reply.
they move on,
ignorant of my meaning.

you're OK right?
they ask another day.
yes, i reply, *i'm okay.*
well, good, they finish.
then they move on.

because how do i explain
how i truly feel?
how do i tell them that i can't sleep
because i'm
overthinking every little detail
of my life?

how do i tell them,
no, i'm not OK, i feel incomplete.
then go on and explain why i feel so?

what words can express
how i feel about myself right now,
shattered, useless, weak, scared,
frustrated, unsure, invisible, pathetic?

if i say that,
i'm wrong
because i should never feel that way.

and they will tell me just that
and explain how i'm
none of those things.

because in their eyes i'm
wonderful and *amazing.*
nothing more.
nothing less.

well, that solves it,
i am OK.
perfectly, wonderfully, amazingly
OK.
because you told me so.
if that's how i should feel,
then i'll pretend to feel that way.

as long as you think i'm OK.
then i'm okay.

thoughts of a teenage girl.

pathetically, uselessly, invisibly
okay.

circles

thoughts wrap around my brain,
repeatedly.
it's a continuous cycle
that never ends.

all of it is a full circle.

it starts with everything being fine
until the mood changes.

where my eyes only see the world
burning.
and rather than put out the flame,
i let it burn.

then the rain comes in
and the world is no longer a glow
now it is black and gloomy
making me feel all alone.

i beg and pray that it will all end
then just when i see the rainbow,
and think my wishes are fulfilled,
the cycle repeats itself.

thoughts of a teenage girl.

forcing me to constantly be
lost in circles.

second place

my heart rapidly beats,
my nerves make my hands shake
then they announce my name.
disappointment sinks in.

i'm given a red ribbon
and i watch the other get blue
i should be proud
but instead, it hurts.

never have i been first
the winner overall
there is always someone
better than me.

and it hurts
it hurts so bad
knowing that i will
never be good enough,
but i have to accept it
because if i don't,
then i'm a sore loser.

i do what i should,
shake the winner's hand,
fake a smile,
and say congratulations.

they pretend to be humble
by saying that i deserved to win,
but they're lying through their teeth
and we both know it.

i know they are grinning
on the inside,
so happy they can barely contain it.
in that moment
wish i was them.

because the only time i win first,
is from being the first loser.
second place,
never good enough for first.

lost

i'm all alone.
it gets hard to breathe.
i can't talk to anyone
because no one is around.

i scream as loud as i can,
but there's not even a sound.
i try to look around,
but everything is dark.

then i realize that i'm lost,
lost in my thoughts
that never seems to go away.

i am now on the street.
crowds of people surround me,
but still, i feel alone.

i realize, once again,
that i am lost.

maybe this is how it will be forever
always lost within myself
and always lost in the world.

thoughts of a teenage girl.

and if i am never found,
just know that i tried to find myself,
yet was unsuccessful.

and if nobody ever finds me,
i guess i'll keep on wandering
in my mind,
in the wild,
lost.

tired

don't wake me up
just let me sleep
because every time i wake up
it's the same old thing.

i'm always tired
of everything all the time.

i'm always exhausted,
trying to figure everything out.

but even when i'm tired,
i have to get up.

i go look in the mirror
and examine the dark circles
under my eyes.

i'm so tired.
so tired of waking up in the morning
with nothing to look forward to.

i'm so tired
of trying to be perfect
when it is impossible
to be just that.

i'm so tired of hearing
the same old thing
day after day.

i want something new,
something worth waking up to.

but nothing ever changes
and, i'm just so tired.
tired.
tired.
tircd.

invisible

as i walk down the hall,
i hope you don't see me
because i can't stand
looking at myself.

i keep my head hung low ,
my eyes focused on my feet.
all i want to be right now is invisible.

i go to the bathroom
and see my reflection in the mirror.
i don't like what i see.
i force myself to keep my eyes away
from my face
because i'm afraid my reflection will
break me.

more than anything
i want to be invisible,
so that i can lift my head high
knowing you can't see me.

thoughts of a teenage girl.

if i were invisible,
i wouldn't care what you'd think
i would dance, jump, twirl, skip,
laugh, and smile
because i wouldn't be afraid.

but no matter how much i wish,
dream, or hope,
it will never come true
you'll always be able to see me.

so, i keep my eyes to the ground
lay down my hair to hide my face
and walk on by
visible for any eye to see.

empty

i try to get up,
i try.
i try.
but today it's hard.

i try to smile.
i try.
i try.
but i cannot do it.

everything feels numb,
empty.

i've lost all motivation.
i've lost all hope.

quiet girl

she looks back and forth
among the crowd
and observes,
yet never says a word.

people walk up to her
and ask, *why are you so quiet?*
she doesn't respond,
yet they keep asking.

it burns her heart,
melts her soul.

she starts to look in the mirror
and hates what she sees
because she's the lonely, quiet girl
with no friends.

when she tries to open up
they ignore her,
but when she stays shut up,
they push her boundaries.

will they ever understand
how lonely she feels?
how hard it is to keep everything
bottled up
when her heart is about to explode?

she thinks that nobody
understands her,
but so many people do.
so many people are in the
exact same situation
who feel just as hopeless
being the quiet girl.

i suck, i suck, i suck

i messed up again.
i suck.
i suck.
i suck.

i'm never good enough.
i suck.
i suck.
i suck.

i lost another friend.
i suck.
i suck.
i suck.

it all went over my head.
i suck.
i suck.
i suck.

i am a horrible person.
i suck.
i suck.
i suck.

repeat

watch.
try.
fail.
learn.

repeat.

watch.
try.
fail.
learn.

repeat.

watch.
try.
fail.
learn.

repeat.

over and over
it's the same process
until the third step
goes from fail
to succeed.

repeat your failures,
continue to try,
continue to experiment,
reason with what you learned,

and repeat.

once you've hit success
keep going
because you'll continue to fail,
yet you'll also continue to succeed.

it was me

i wonder why i'm so sad
and i look for something—
someone
to put the blame on
for all of my misery.

but then i realize,
it was me the whole time.
i was the one
hurting myself.

i told myself that i was obnoxious,
so, i stopped talking.
hiding my inner child away
from the rest of the world
because i'm supposed to grow up.

i was only twelve.

i told myself that everyone cared
about what i looked like,
so i became self-conscious,
comparing myself to women
much older than myself.

i was only a child.

i told myself that i wasn't
good enough,
so i became a perfectionist,
pushing myself harder
and punishing myself
if i didn't succeed.

why is everyone so much
better than me?

i told myself that i loved myself,
so i became delusional,
turning what was once the truth
into a lie.

and yet i still wonder
why am i so sad?

overthinking

constant thoughts
go through my mind
night and day
making me restless.

i manage to turn
the simplest things
into a complex pile of anxiety
just by falling in a rabbit hole
of *what ifs* and scenarios.

i'm always nervous
that something bad
is going to happen
even though
there is no sign of danger.

i can't fall asleep
because i think of all the things
i did
and didn't do.

small details from my day
i replay,
picking out all the mistakes i made

and how much it affected
everyone else.

i remember
the embarrassing, frustrating,
difficult moments i have lived
and have tried to forget
but never did.

it sucks.

it sucks to care so much.
it sucks to think so much.
especially when that's all i ever do.

too much

it is all too much
and it's freaking me out,
but what can i do?

i thought i could take it
but in all, i can't
my mind was hungry
but my plate was already full.
it's too much.

i can't quit
that's not right,
but how can i keep going?

it's too much, i'm telling you
i can't go on.
everything has gone wrong,
and i don't know what to do.

it's too much for me to handle.
this isn't how it ought to be.
somehow, i managed
to tangle my life into a knot
i struggle to untie.

and no one will help me
because no one can fix it
except me.

if i got myself into this mess,
how can i get out?

it's all too much
it's all too much.
it's all too much!

now, i'm freaking out
because this stupid knot
won't untie.

too much, i'm telling you…
it's all too much…

will i get out…
will i get help…
too much, too much…

realization

everything starts to glitch.
my vision starts to blur.
panic sets in.

words become blank.
my focus is lost.
my head starts to ache.
nothing makes sense.

darkness is my friend.
the light is an enemy.
time slows down.
nothing matters.

sleep takes a long time to come.
once it does,
i'm gone.

then i wake up.
no longer aching.
no longer breaking.
no longer in fear.

realization sinks in.

everything is just silent.

thoughts of a teenage girl.

and instantly,
my mind begins to apologize
to my body
for the miscommunication
that everything is okay.

because everything is *not* okay,
and there has to be a way
to turn this around.

there has to be a solution
to all the stress,
all the thinking,
all the exhaustion
that is constantly wrapped
around me.

if there is not,
then things will get worse
and i'll drown
in my own troubled waters
never to rise again.

actually happy

i strike a match
and let the flame burn
the wick of the candle.

the sweet smell of lavender
fills my lungs
and immediately
i feel calm.

i put a record on,
listening to the lyrics of the songs
on my favorite album.

my fingers fly
over my keyboard,
clicking the keys where
i pour my heart out
onto a page.

my words keep me satisfied.

my heart is alive again.
my mind is free.
my soul is happy.
my body is clean.

right now, everything is perfect.

i'm actually content,
actually focused,
actually *happy*.

message in a bottle

there is someone out there
who feels just like i did
last week.

exhausted, stressed, frustrated…
and i know
i'll repeat a week like that again.

if i could write
a message in a bottle
from where i am right now,
finally at peace from the cycle,
i would tell those struggling, this:

focus on yourself.
take a break from social media.
do something you love.
enjoy every moment.

your problems
won't be solved overnight,
but wasting your time
hurting yourself
won't be worth it.

thoughts of a teenage girl.

little did i know
i was the one
who needed that message
the most.

up i grow

am i ready?
no.
but time won't stop
for a young girl
about to be a woman.

i can't get any younger,
so up i grow
in age,
in mistakes,
in memories.

i never thought i'd actually
be this close,
yet i stand corrected
because here i am
on the edge of my childhood
about to begin the unknown.

you can't exactly
predict the unknown
you can plan it,
but plans constantly change.

thoughts of a teenage girl.

i don't know where
i'll be a year from now,
or two years,
or five years.

all i know
is that i can't stop the minutes
from flying by.

so i guess up i grow
taking a step into the unknown.

loser

i've never been invited to parties.
i'd always hear about them,
but not in too much detail.

i don't go to sleepovers
or have anyone over at my house.
i usually just hang out
alone after school
reading and writing.

i only have a couple of friends,
and those who don't really know me,
think that i don't have any.

i don't date
because boys aren't into me.
maybe i'm unapproachable,
or just kind of ugly.

my mom is my best friend.
i never do anything wrong.
i am a weirdo.
i sing random songs
when i'm nervous.

thoughts of a teenage girl.

i try to make friends
by embarrassing myself
hoping that they'll like me,
but it never works.

i've tried being myself
in order to make friends,
but that doesn't work either.

in all honesty,
i'm a *loser*
and i accept that.

when did it all change?

when did everything change?
and when did i become
foreign to an atmosphere
which i used to thrive in?

how long will this last?
the awkward moments
of not knowing what to say
when one you know— *love,*
pours every heartbreaking detail
about what they are going through
to you,
and you're just
silent?

it's easier to distract myself
because i silently pray
that by the time i bring myself back
something will change,
something will be better.

and everytime i see a spark of hope
in which *something* has changed for
the better,
it's easily blown away
by a gust of wind.

i feel disconnected.
i feel like i don't know
anything anymore,
but i should.
i really should.

none of it makes sense.
when did it all change?

music

the lyrics
that i never understood
when i was younger
are now the rhythm
of my heartbeat.

the instruments
all work together
in order to create
a beautiful melody
which blithely flows
through my ears.

isn't it crazy
how much music
impacts my life?

some prefer silence.
some hate the music i love.
some think that good music has died,
don't worry, i'll keep it alive.

thoughts of a teenage girl.

i'll sing my heart out
when the radio plays
my favorite song
even if i sound atrocious
because i *love* it.

if i'm crying,
music will be my comfort,
because every lyric
seems to express exactly how i feel.

music might as well
be a part of my bloodstream
because i can't live without it
and i won't dare to let it die.

embarrassment

with every step i take
i manage to slip and fall
right on my face
in the middle of the hall.

people stop and stare,
poorly attempting to hold in
their laughter
and they fail,
making me want to sink
six feet underground.

anymore,
i don't just have my occasional
embarrassing moments.
it's an everyday occurrence.

i am always awkward
trying to talk to people
that i don't know.

i stutter and mispronounce my words
even though
i should know how to speak clearly.

i wave and smile at the group of girls
who were waving to the person
behind me.
i turn around
realizing that i'm an idiot.

i'm just a walking disaster
of embarrassment.

in all reality

in all reality,
i talk to myself.

i pretend i'm in an interview
for a famous book i wrote.

i talk in different accents,
making myself laugh.

i talk to an imaginary camera
about all my hopes and dreams.

i talk to myself
to keep myself company.

in all reality
i dance and sing
in my bathroom alone
because i think it's fun.

i sing in the shower,
convincing myself that i sing
masterfully
until i try to hit a high note
which i fail, miserably.

but it's okay
because that's all me.

in all reality
i am shy at first,
but once you get to know me
i'm a social butterfly.

i make awful jokes,
have a ridiculous laugh,
and dance to the beat
of my own drum.

oh, and if you say a word
that's in a song,
i'll be singing it all day long
without any shame.

in all reality
i'm a hopeless romantic
who has such high expectations,
although i've never even held hands.

i love to read,
i love to write,
and i think about the word, *love*,
all the time.

in all reality
i'm a goofy girl
who still feels like the kid
who wanted to be princess peach
in kindergarten.

in all reality
i have many flaws
which i point out, constantly.

in all reality
i have many strengths
which i tend to overlook.

in all reality
i hate being lonely,
but i can make it
on my own.

in all reality
i'm an angsty teenage girl
who has too many hobbies to count,
and who struggles
communicating with others.

so, i wrote a poem to tell you all
about who i am
in all reality.

do you know me now?

as i write these poems,
i express everything that
i have been feeling.
i am now an open book
that you have read.

so, do you know me now?

i was the quiet kid.
i didn't talk much.
have i given you enough reasons
to understand why?

from what you have read
can you see my dreams
and how much i want
to achieve them?

do you understand now
why i am the way i am?
how i feel bad on some days
and good on others?

all i've ever wanted
was to express myself,
and have you understand
exactly how i feel.

how my mind
and my thoughts
work in circles.

the way my mood shifts
from left to right
within seconds.

and how much
i wanted to be your friend.
i wanted that so so so much,
but i just couldn't express it.

tell me,
do you know me now?

dear reader

if you picked up this book,
flipped through the pages,
and read the words,
then thank you.

if you relate to the things i've said,
just know that you are not alone.

i have listened all of my life
to other people's stories.
all i've ever wanted
was to tell mine.

and if you want to tell your story,
do it.
i will listen.

i want to let you know,
my dear reader,
that you are amazing.

you have so many great things
just waiting to happen,
but why wait?

make it happen.

i believe in you.
push yourself,
but not too hard.

if you need to take a break,
take one.
if you need more time,
take it.

don't rush,
just start
because the sooner you start
the closer you'll be
to achieving your dreams.

once again,
dear reader,
thank you for your time
to help make my dream
a reality.

and whatever i can do in return,
just let me know
and i will try my best
to return the favor.

thoughts of a teenage girl.

my dear reader,
thank you.

katherine mazzei

thoughts of a teenage girl.

katherine mazzei

a poet's

notes

Why Muse cl line in such a lonely World?

Everyone loves a Rose
until they get pricked
by the thorn.

If I could view myself from your eyes, What would I See?

I am Weeping ~
because I am unable to
embrace my unalluring
Conterance bestowed upon
civilization.

Desperate for Something
that'll mean nothing
Desperate . . .

Don't they know that boys aren't the only one's who can break your heart? I've been breaking mine for years, So that I won't have to feel the pain later on.

I've got ink stains on my fingers from writing letters to you. But you'll never get to read what I poured my heart and soul into.

You take shots in the
dark You get bruses.

I striked all the matches,
but never got a flame.

you are a stone
that gracefully skips
across the water. I am
just a rock that sinks to
the bottom.

thoughts of a teenage girl.

Thoughts are like a piece of elastic, how far can you stretch them until they snap?

A light wouldn't
shine without
darkness.

thoughts of a teenage girl.

~~Fuck, Damn. Shit, Bitch~~
No. those words shall
not express non discribe
my hate, agression, or
frustration.
I shall take a much more
creative approch . . .

katherine mazzei

thoughts of a teenage girl.

acknowledgements

Oh, where to begin! I want to start off by thanking my friends and family for their undying support throughout this entire process. It has been hard, but the kind words of encouragement I have received from y'all have been able to keep me going. I especially want to thank my mom, my favorite person in the entire world. Thank you for reading my manuscript over and over again throughout this process, your feedback, your love, and your support is the greatest thing that I can receive. I appreciate and love you.

I want to thank my teachers for reading my manuscript and providing me with honest feedback. I hold such high respect for you all and your opinions truly matter to me. One teacher I would like to thank in particular is Mrs. Orchard. Without taking your creative writing class, I would have never been introduced to writing poetry and finally being able to express myself as well as pursue my dreams. You may not know

your impact on my writing, but I sure do.
Thank you so much.

Lastly, I would like to thank the
Bookstagram community and all of my beta
readers who have taken the time to read my
book or share it with others. Being a part of
this community has been one of the greatest
decisions I have made. Not only have I
grown as a reader, but I have also grown as
a writer. I love and thank you all! ♥

katherine mazzei

thoughts of a teenage girl.

about the author

Katherine Mazzei is a sixteen-year-old author and was born in Johnson City, Tennessee. Her spark of interest in writing began when she won 1ˢᵗ place in her school's forensics competition under the category of prose. Since then, she has written numerous short stories and unfinished manuscripts in hopes of becoming an author someday. In her junior year of high school, she began writing poetry to cope with her stress and emotions. That's when she decided to write, *thoughts of a teenage girl,* in hopes of inspiring and assuring that other girls her age are not alone. *thoughts of a teenage girl* is Katherine's first book, of what she hopes to be, many more.